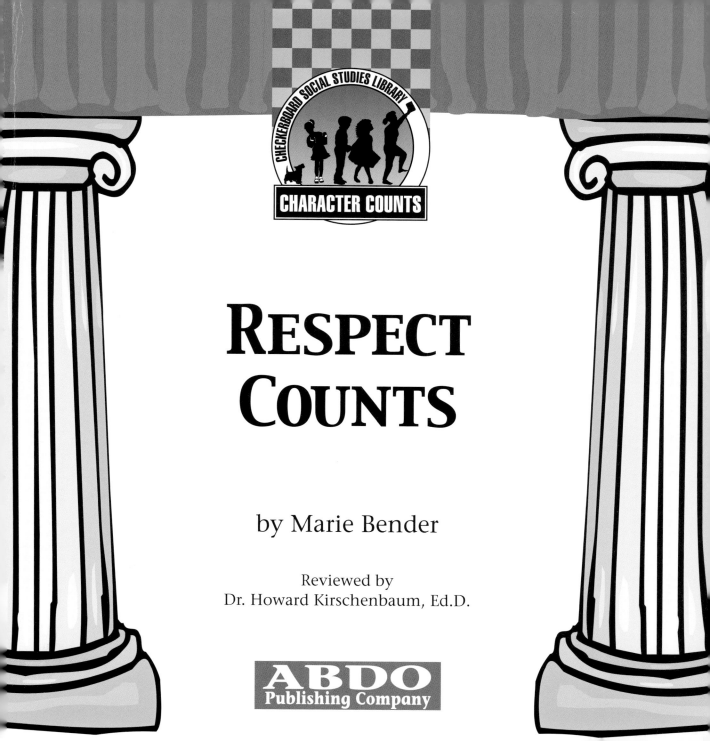

CHECKERBOARD SOCIAL STUDIES LIBRARY

CHARACTER COUNTS

RESPECT COUNTS

by Marie Bender

Reviewed by
Dr. Howard Kirschenbaum, Ed.D.

ABDO
Publishing Company

Published by ABDO Publishing Company, 4940 Viking Drive, Edina, Minnesota 55435. Copyright ©
2003 by Abdo Consulting Group, Inc. International copyrights reserved in all countries. No part of
this book may be reproduced in any form without written permission from the publisher.

Printed in the United States

Photo credits: BananaStock Ltd., Comstock, Eyewire Images, Image 100, PhotoDisc,
      Skjold Photography

Editors: Kate A. Conley, Stephanie Hedlund

Design and production: Mighty Media

Library of Congress Cataloging-in-Publication Data

Bender, Marie, 1968-
    Respect counts / Marie Bender.
      p. cm. -- (Character counts)
    Summary: Defines respect as a character trait and discusses how to show respect at
home, with friends, at school, in the community, and toward oneself.
    Includes bibliographical references (p.) and index.
    ISBN 1-57765-873-6
    1. Respect--Juvenile literature. [1. Respect.] I. Title.

BJ1533.R4 B46 2002
179'.9--dc21

                                             2002066693

Internationally known educator and author Howard Kirschenbaum has worked with schools,
non-profit organizations, governmental agencies, and private businesses around the world to
develop school/family/community relations and values education programs for more than 30
years. He has written more than 20 books about character education, including a high school
curriculum. Dr. Kirschenbaum is currently the Frontier Professor of School, Family, and
Community Relations at the University of Rochester and teaches classes in counseling and
human development.

CONTENTS

CHARACTER COUNTS

All people are created equal.

—*Thomas Jefferson, third president of the United States*

Your character is the combination of **traits** that makes you an individual. It's not your physical traits, such as the color of your eyes or how tall you are. Rather, character is your thoughts, feelings, beliefs, and values.

Your character shows in the way you interact with your family, friends, teachers, and other community members. People who are well liked and successful are said to have a good character. Many traits build good character. Some of these traits include caring, fairness, honesty, good citizenship, responsibility, and respect.

Good Citizenship

Respect Responsibility Honesty

Fairness Caring

Respect Counts

James was working on a school report that was due the next day. His dad came to his room and said, "James! The kitchen is a mess! It's your job to do the dishes after dinner. I want you to do them right now!"

James knew that doing the dishes was his job. But he hadn't done them because he had to finish the report. James had hoped his dad would realize that he hadn't ignored his responsibility just to goof off.

James was upset that his dad had yelled at him. But instead of yelling back or slamming his book closed and stomping to the kitchen, James said, "Dad, I'm sorry I didn't do the dishes. I thought it was more important to finish my homework—this report is due tomorrow. Would it be okay if I got up early and did the dishes before I go to school?"

His dad said, "Yes, that would be okay this time."

James made respect count.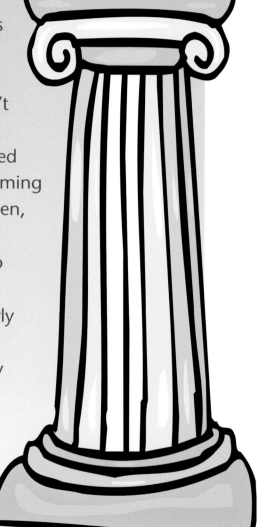

WHAT IS RESPECT?

If you respect others, there will be peace.

—Benito Juárez, former president of Mexico

Respect can mean many things. It means believing that everyone deserves to be treated fairly and politely. It also means believing that all human beings have worth. Respect is treating others the way you want to be treated. It means showing consideration for the environment, authority, **elders**, and yourself.

The Golden Rule
Around the World

Hurt not others in ways that you yourself would find hurtful. —Buddha

So whatever you wish that men would do to you, do so to them; for this is the law and the prophets. —*The Gospel of Matthew*

Do not do to others what you do not want them to do to you. —Confucius

Do naught unto others which would cause you pain if done to you. —*The Mahabarata*

No one of you is a believer until he desires for his brother that which he desires for himself. —Muhammad

What is hateful to you, do not to your fellow man. —*The Talmud*

Regard your neighbor's gain as your own gain, and your neighbor's loss as your own loss. —Tai Shang Kan Ying P'ien

There are many ways to show respect. One way is to be **tolerant** and accepting of others. There are many different languages, **customs**, and beliefs. So not everyone looks, thinks, or feels the same way you do. But that doesn't mean they are wrong. They are just different. Believing that something different is bad or wrong is disrespectful.

You can respect differences by talking, listening, and sharing with others. The more you learn about others, the easier it is to understand and accept them. Respect doesn't mean you always have to agree. You can have your own opinions, and people should respect your right to disagree. But if you disagree with someone, you can do so respectfully, without fighting or name-calling. Other people have as much right to their opinions as you do to yours.

Having good manners is another way of showing respect. Using polite words, such as *please*, *thank you*, and *excuse me*, shows respect. Doing polite things, such as opening doors for others or waiting your turn in line, shows that you are considerate. People are more likely to respect you if you are polite. Being rude, shouting, or demanding things is impolite and disrespectful.

> Think about it...
>
> *How do you feel when you have been disrespected?*
>
> *What does it teach you about how to treat others?*

Accepting others for who they are is respectful behavior. And everyone, including you, deserves to be treated politely. If everyone treated each other equally and politely, there would be no **prejudice** or hate.

Think about it...

What are good manners?

Why are they important?

RESPECT AND FAMILY

A good person respects others.

—Desmond Tutu, South African religious leader

You probably spend a lot of time with your family. They are the people you know best, and who know you best. Because you know them so well, sometimes it is hard to remember that they deserve to be treated with respect, too. But they should always be treated kindly and politely, not only because they are family, but also because everyone should be treated with respect.

Respect is displayed in different ways with different members of your family. You respect your parents by following their rules and doing what they ask. You respect your **siblings** by knocking before going into their rooms and asking to use their things. Showing respect for your family also provides a considerate way to deal with conflicts.

Pets deserve to be treated with respect, too. They are part of your family and rely on you to

Think about it...

How do you treat things that belong to others?

Do you care for them as you do for your own things?

provide them with a safe place to live. You respect your pet by not playing with it when it is trying to eat. You also respect your pet by not teasing it. It is disrespectful to scare or hurt animals for any reason.

RESPECT AND FRIENDS

*We all have to live here together. Respect each other and
see the best in each other.* —Colin Powell, U.S. secretary of state

Your friends are people you choose to spend time with. If you didn't respect them, they wouldn't be your friends. If they didn't respect you, you wouldn't be their friend either.

You probably have a lot in common with your friends. You like to do many of the same things, and you have fun together. But there are also

differences between you. Respecting your friends means showing you have an interest in the things that are important to them. You don't always have to agree with your friends. But listening to their feelings, thoughts, and ideas shows you respect them.

Part of respecting others means accepting their right to have opinions that are different than yours. It is important to talk about differences and try to understand why your friends feel the way they do. It is okay to disagree about some things. Everyone is entitled to their own opinions and choices as long as their actions do not harm others. Respecting your friends means not teasing them or calling them names because of their opinions.

Respecting your friends also means sharing your things with them and taking care of the things they share with you. Respecting your friends' property shows that you care about your friends and what is important to them. This is part of being friends, and it is also part of being respectful.

How do you react when you and your friends disagree?

Do you think you are always right?

How can you act respectfully in these situations?

RESPECT

RESPECT AND SCHOOL

Never look down on anybody unless you're helping him up.

—Jesse Jackson, political activist and preacher

Being respectful at school means showing respect for authority. Authority figures include teachers, principals, and other staff members. They make rules to provide a safe place for everybody at your school. By following their rules, you show you respect them and value their time and experience.

Some teachers have specific rules in addition to general school rules. It is your responsibility to follow these rules. This will make your classroom a better place to learn. When you act respectfully, your classmates may follow your lead.

It is also important to respect your classmates. Many of your classmates look, think, and act differently than you. Respecting your classmates means accepting them and not teasing them or putting them down because they seem different. If you get to know them better, you may find you have things in common, too. You might even become friends.

Respecting your classmates also means respecting their right to learn. If you finish a test or assignment early, sit quietly until everyone is finished.

RESPECT

17

Being **disruptive** in class does not help anyone learn. If another student does not understand something that you think is easy, offer to explain it to your classmate rather than teasing him or her. Someday, someone may return this favor to you.

It is also important to respect school property. Schools spend a lot of money to provide supplies and equipment for their students. Many students think it is okay to write on walls, desks, books, or lockers or to steal things that belong to the school. But this is disrespectful. You have the right to use school property when you attend the school or participate in activities. It is respectful to take care of these things as if they were your own.

How can you show respect at school?

How do you feel when people respect you?

RESPECT

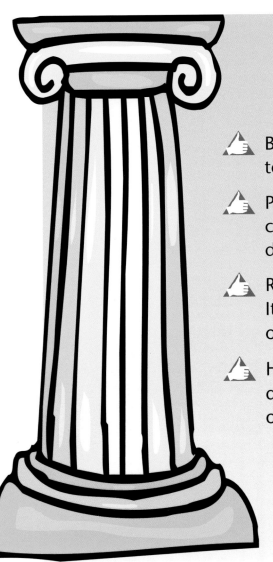

School Rules

Do . . .

Be on time to class. It is disrespectful to disrupt class by coming in late.

Pay attention to the teacher during class. It is disrespectful to daydream or doodle when the teacher is talking.

Raise your hand to talk in class. It is disrespectful to interrupt others or to speak out of turn.

Help others when needed. It is disrespectful to ignore the needs of others if you can help.

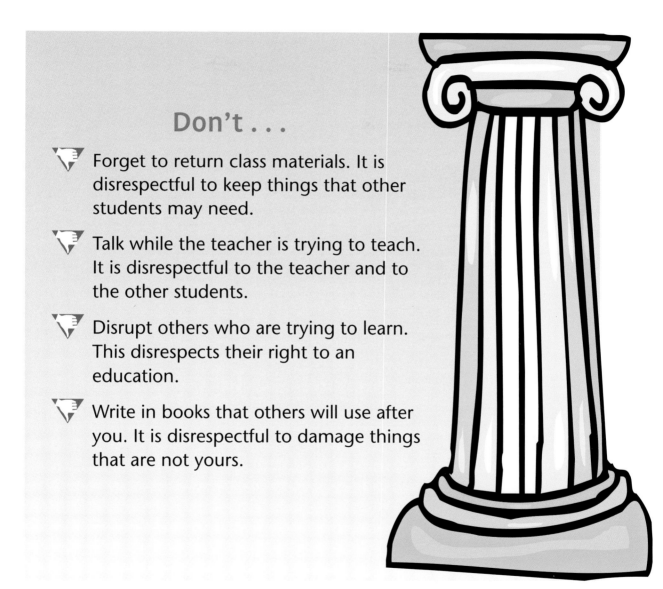

Don't . . .

▽ Forget to return class materials. It is disrespectful to keep things that other students may need.

▽ Talk while the teacher is trying to teach. It is disrespectful to the teacher and to the other students.

▽ Disrupt others who are trying to learn. This disrespects their right to an education.

▽ Write in books that others will use after you. It is disrespectful to damage things that are not yours.

21

RESPECT AND COMMUNITY

Respect for right conduct is felt by every body.

—Jane Austen, novelist

Respecting your community means obeying its laws. Elected officials, such as the mayor, council members, and other lawmakers, determine laws in your community. But the laws are for everyone to follow. They exist to help make your community a safe place for everyone. People in authority, such as police officers and firefighters, enforce community laws.

Your community is made up of many different people. Some of them you may know very well. You recognize others because you have seen them at the store or at the park. Some are complete strangers. But all of the people in your community should be treated equally and respectfully.

It's the Law . . .

 Cross streets at intersections and crosswalks only. It is not only disrespectful, but also dangerous to make cars stop suddenly or swerve to miss you.

 Walk your dog on a leash and pick up its droppings. It is disrespectful to dirty people's yards or public areas.

 Pedestrians have the right of way when crossing the street. It is disrespectful to ride your bike through a crosswalk without waiting for pedestrians to cross.

 Wear a helmet when bicycling, skateboarding, or in-line skating. It is disrespectful not to protect yourself from injury.

RESPECT

You also respect your community by caring for the environment. There are many ways you can help create a clean, safe place to live. **Recycling** cans, bottles, and paper at home and school reduces waste. Picking up litter in the park is also a good way to take care of the environment and your neighborhood. So is using **organic** household cleaners or keeping harmful chemicals out of the water and air. If we don't respect our environment, our communities will become less safe and less attractive.

Ways to Reduce, Reuse, Recycle, and Respect

 Use old newspaper as gift wrapping.

 Plant a garden or a tree.

 Use recycled paper.

 Take your lunch in a reusable lunch box, thermos, and sandwich container instead of using cans and paper and plastic bags.

 Use environmentally safe products.

 Give items you no longer use to charity.

RESPECT

SELF-RESPECT

Self-respect has nothing to do with the approval of others.

—Joan Didion, author

Don't forget that you deserve respect, too. You deserve respect from other people, as well as from yourself. You can show self-respect by taking care of your body. Brushing your teeth, exercising, getting proper sleep, and eating healthy foods are ways to respect your body. It is important to take care of yourself so you can be healthy.

You can also show respect for your mind. To do this, you can try your best at school. If you do not understand something, you can ask your teacher, parent, or older **sibling** to explain it until you do understand. It's okay to ask for help. It shows that you care enough about yourself that you are not afraid to ask for what you need.

You show respect for your feelings by standing up for yourself. Respecting other people's feelings does not mean you deny your own. If people say or do something that hurts you, you can tell them that you don't like it, and ask them to stop. If they don't stop, you can go to a parent, teacher, or other adult for help. You deserve to be treated respectfully.

Respecting yourself also means liking who you are. Sometimes you might wish you were smarter, better looking, or more athletic. But liking yourself means accepting who you are. You can change some things about yourself if you really want to, but there are other things you cannot change. Respecting yourself means believing in yourself and your abilities.

Why is it important to like yourself?

What are some ways you can show you respect yourself?

RESPECT AND ELDERS

Not until just before dawn do people sleep best; not until people get old do they become wise. — *Chinese proverb*

In many **cultures**, **elders** receive extra respect. In these cultures, life experience is highly valued. Elderly people are considered a source of wisdom and strength.

It is easy to think that because things today seem so different from when your grandparents were young they won't be able to understand what you face. But remember, they have a lot of wisdom because they have many years of life experience. They may be able to relate to you more than you realize.

There are many ways to respect your **elders**. If you are on a crowded bus, you can give your seat to an older person so he or she will not have to stand. You can help an elderly neighbor carry groceries, rake leaves, or take out the trash. When you spend time with your grandparents or elders in your community, ask them what life was like when they were growing up. You may be surprised at how many experiences you have in common.

Think about it...

Is it hard to talk with older people?

How can you show you respect their feelings and beliefs?

RESPECT

Glossary

culture - the customs, arts, and tools of a nation or people at a certain time.

custom - an accepted social habit or behavior of a group.

disrupt - to throw into disorder.

elder - a person having authority because of age or experience.

organic - of, using, or grown without benefit of chemical fertilizers or insecticides.

prejudice - an often negative opinion formed without knowing all the facts.

recycle - to make suitable for reuse.

sibling - a brother or sister.

tolerant - willing to accept other people's behaviors or customs.

trait - a quality that distinguishes one person or group from another.

Web Sites

Would you like to learn more about character? Please visit www.abdopub.com to find up-to-date Web site links about caring, fairness, honesty, good citizenship, responsibility, and respect. These links are routinely monitored and updated to provide the most current information available.

INDEX

For the Character Counts series, ABDO Publishing Company researched leading character education resources and references in an effort to present accurate information about developing good character and why doing so is important. While the title of the series is Character Counts, these books do not represent the Character Counts organization or its mission. ABDO Publishing Company recognizes and thanks the numerous organizations that provide information and support for building good character in school, at home, and in the community.